LIFE ON A SHEEP FARM

LIFE ON A SHEEP FARM

by Judy Wolfman
photographs by David Lorenz Winston

LIFE ON A FARM

Carolrhoda Books, Inc. / Minneapolis

Many thanks to the members of the Bates family—Anne, Randy, Diana, and Grandma Anne—
for allowing us to visit their farm and providing valuable information about their sheep.

—J.W. and D.L.W.

Text copyright © 2004 by Judy Wolfman
Photographs copyright © 2004 by David Lorenz Winston

Carolrhoda Books, Inc.
A division of Lerner Publishing Group
241 First Avenue North
Minneapolis, MN 55401 U.S.A.

Website address: www.lernerbooks.com

Library of Congress Cataloging-in-Publication Data

Wolfman, Judy.
    Life on a sheep farm / by Judy Wolfman ; photographs by David Lorenz
Winston.
        p.   cm. — (Life on a farm)
    Summary: Explains the activities that take place on a working sheep farm,
from the perspective of a child who lives there.
    Includes index.
    ISBN: 1–57505–192–3 (lib. bdg. : alk. paper)
    1. Sheep—Juvenile literature. 2. Sheep ranches—Juvenile literature.
3. Farm life—Juvenile literature. [1. Sheep. 2. Sheep ranches. 3. Farm life.]
I. Winston, David Lorenz, ill. II. Title.
SF375.2.W65 2004
636.3—dc21   2002154718

Manufactured in the United States of America
1 2 3 4 5 6 – JR – 09 08 07 06 05 04

CONTENTS

GRANDMA'S Sheep Farm

One of my favorite sheep eats from my hand.

Some people count sheep to help them fall asleep, but I count them because I spend lots of time on a sheep farm. My name is Diana Bates. My family and I help my grandmother raise sheep on her farm. It's called the Arasapha Farm.

Along with my parents, I have three sisters and two brothers. We live on the same land as my grandma, but we have our own house on our own farm. We grow vegetables and raise lots of animals

there. Mom and Dad do most of the work. That way, we kids can help Grandma out when she needs it. We work on her sheep farm after school, on weekends, and during school breaks. Her house is close to ours, on top of the hill. We can easily walk there.

6

I love helping Grandma raise her sheep on her beautiful farm.

7

This is a Shropshire. I think it's neat that its ears are always sticking out!

Most sheep farmers raise sheep for their wool or for food. On my grandma's farm, we raise sheep for both reasons. The kind of sheep we raise are called Shropshire. A Shropshire's body is covered with white wool, and it has a short tail. Its legs are bulky and dark from the knee down. Its head is white, with a dark face. Long, dark ears stand out from the sides of its head. I think Shropshires are very pretty.

When I'm not feeding the sheep, I like to play with them and pet them.

Some sheep touch my nose with theirs. It feels like they're kissing me!

Sheep like to slowly follow each other around the pastures. But if you try to catch one, it can run really fast!

Grandma usually has about seventy **ewes**, or female sheep, and three **rams**, or male sheep. Most of the time, we keep the sheep in three pastures, or grassy fields. The sheep we use for wool, we keep for a long time. The sheep we sell for meat, we have for about six months, from the time they're born until they have to leave the farm.

Once in a while, I get to show my sheep at county and **4-H** fairs. I'm a member of 4-H. This organization helps kids learn skills and explore different careers. Kids who are part of 4-H work on projects, such as raising and showing sheep.

I have to train the sheep for showing at local fairs.

Getting a sheep ready for show is a lot of work! While I brush her wool and trim her hooves, my sheep waits patiently in a special stand.

Sometimes I have to wash the sheep before I show, too.

Once in a while at fairs, I win a ribbon or a trophy. When that happens, I give each winning sheep a big hug!

At fairs, our sheep are judged. Sometimes they're judged on how well groomed they are and how well they walk and stand. Other times, the sheep are judged on the way they look, compared to other Shropshires. The sheep I show, I keep for a long time. I have one sheep that's nine years old!

When I'm not showing sheep, I like to help Grandma by working on the farm. I feed the sheep, make sure they stay healthy, and keep them comfortable. But helping to bring a baby sheep, or **lamb**, into the world is one of my favorite jobs.

Here's a mother sheep with her little lamb.

I like to take care of Grandma's sheep and keep them healthy.

WELCOME

Little Lambs

It won't be long before this yearling will be ready for breeding.

Since we sell many of the sheep for meat, we always need more lambs. Every August, we **breed** our sheep, or help them become pregnant. We breed ewes that have already had lambs. We also breed young ewes that haven't given birth yet. These ewes are called **yearlings** and are just over one year old. After a yearling has her first lamb, we breed her every year. Some ewes breed for eight years. That's a lot of lambs for one ewe!

When it's time to breed, we put a group of ewes in each of our pastures. Then we put a ram with each group. When a ewe starts to rub against a ram, that means she's ready for breeding.

Two months later, we can tell if she's **settled**, or pregnant. Her belly gets bigger, and her **udder** gets larger. An udder is where the ewe stores the milk she'll make for her lambs.

While these rams wait to meet the ewes, they keep busy by eating and walking around the pasture.

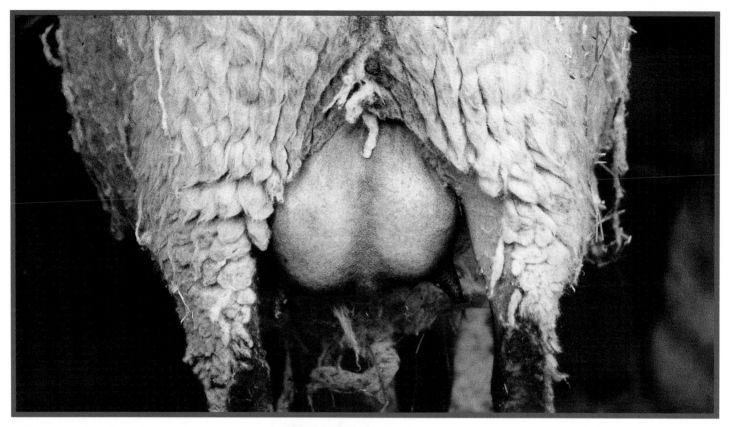

This ewe's udder is getting ready to make lots of milk for her baby.

Once a ewe is bred, she's pregnant for about five months. Those months go fast. We can't wait for the babies to be born! About two weeks before a ewe gives birth, we give her a shot in the leg. This shot protects her and her unborn lamb from getting sick.

In January or February, the ewe's body begins to change. Her udder gets larger and harder. The underside of her tail gets pink and swollen, too. When we see these signs, we know she is getting ready to **lamb**, or give birth. Some sheep will give birth very soon. Others may take three or four weeks before they lamb.

When the ewe is closer to giving birth, one of us leads her from the pasture into the barn. She'll be more comfortable in the barn. It's warm and dry, and there's soft hay she can rest on. We have about twelve stalls in the barn. These stalls are for ewes that are ready to give birth. They are called **lambing pens**.

Soon this ewe will go into the barn to have her little lamb.

19

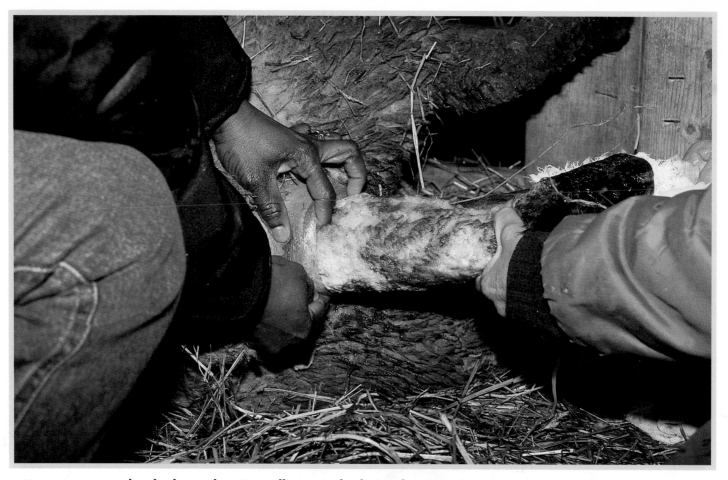

I've seen many lambs born, but I'm still amazed when it happens!

When the ewe finally begins to lamb, the babies are born in fifteen to twenty minutes. Our ewes usually have twins, which is common. But once in a while, a ewe will have triplets!

After the lambs are born, we use a towel to wipe the **mucus** from their mouths and bodies. Mucus is a slippery coating that covers a newborn lamb's body. Sometimes Grandma picks a lamb up by its hind legs and shakes it a little bit. The mucus just falls right off.

20

After the newborn lamb is born, my sister Katie holds it in her arms and wipes it off with a soft towel.

This mother and baby are meeting each other for the first time. They'll have time to bond now.

A newborn lamb is adorable. It enters the world with its eyes open. It weighs about 7 pounds and is usually 14 inches long from head to tail. That's about the size of a large puppy.

There's a lot to do after a lamb is born. First we take special care of the **umbilical cord**. Before birth, this cord was the lifeline between the mother and baby. The cord breaks when the lamb is born, but a piece of it is still attached to the lamb. To prevent an infection, we dip the cord into a special liquid. This liquid keeps germs away. (In two or three days, the cord will dry up and fall off.)

The lamb doesn't seem to mind when Katie dips its umbilical cord in the special liquid.

About one hour after a lamb is born, its wobbly legs start straightening up. Before we know it, the little lamb is standing! After about fifteen minutes, the lamb is walking all around the barn.

I think it's amazing that lambs can walk so soon after they're born.
This one prances around like it's been walking for weeks!

These lambs are hanging out with their mother in the pasture.

It's hard to believe that these little lambs will be as big as their mother one day.

This lamb knows exactly what to do when it's hungry.

By this time, the lamb is hungry. It starts to look for its mother's **teat**, or nipple. Sometimes it doesn't look in the right direction, so we have to help it find its way. Once the lamb finds its mother's teat, it begins to **nurse**, or drink milk. (Since sheep have two teats, twin lambs can nurse at the same time.)

For the first twenty-four hours of its life, a lamb drinks **colostrum** from its mother. Colostrum is thick milk that is loaded with vitamins and minerals. It's very important that a lamb gets colostrum right away, so it has a healthy start. After the first day, the lamb still drinks its mother's milk. It's just thinner than the colostrum.

Three days after the lamb is born, it still nurses in the lambing pen. At this time, we put a tag through one of its ears. The tag has an identification number on it. It also tells us who the lamb's mother and father are. Getting a tag doesn't hurt any more than getting an ear pierced.

This mother sheep is a walking milk machine!

This lamb will need to get its tail docked soon.

The same day we give the lamb an ear tag, we **dock** its tail. Docking means taking a lamb's tail off, but this doesn't hurt the lamb. We do this because flies can stick to the lamb's tail and backside. The germs they carry can make the lamb sick. To dock the lamb's tail, we put a rubber band around it. In a couple of weeks, the tail falls off. Once it's gone, it doesn't grow back. Docking is important to keep the lamb clean and healthy.

We let the lambs and ewes stay in the lambing pens for four or five days. After that, the lambs are ready to live outside. We put the lambs and their mothers into an area where they can eat hay and feed. Feed is a mixture of corn that we grow and oats and soybean meal that we buy. We also add molasses to the feed, which makes it taste sweet. Even though the lambs eat the feed, they mostly drink milk from their mother.

We keep the feed in this container. It holds enough to feed our sheep for a couple of days.

These lambs are getting used to living on their own.

We **wean** the lambs from their mother after about two months of nursing. Weaning trains the lambs to stop drinking milk. It's time for them to start eating more solid foods, like feed. To wean a lamb, we separate the lamb and its mother by putting them in two different pastures. Sometimes, we hear them call out to each other. It makes us a little sad to hear this.

Just like people, sheep have their own voices. Some are high, and some are low. Some say maaa, and some say baaa. Their voices shake a little when they call out. If they all talk at once, the sounds are so loud we have to wear earplugs!

I think the sheep make their sounds so they can talk to each other.

These two lambs are taking a little afternoon stroll together.

A week after we separate a lamb and its mother, the lamb is quieter and doesn't seem to miss nursing. Without its mother's milk, the growing lamb eats more feed. Lambs eat out of creep feeders. These feeders are in an area with a small gate. To get to the feeder, lambs creep through a small opening. The lambs can eat anytime, but the small opening keeps out the bigger sheep.

When a lamb eats, sometimes it doesn't know when to stop. If it eats too much, it can get overeating disease. When this happens, a lamb's stomach gets really full. This can cause it to die. When the lambs start eating from the creep feeders, we give the lamb a shot to prevent this disease.

Lambs are half grown by the time they are six months old. (They weigh between 75 and 100 pounds.) Now it's time to say good-bye to the ones we have to sell. It's hard for me to think about sending them away. But it makes me feel good to know the sheep will feed a lot of people.

We always keep about ten of our female lambs. We can use these lambs to make more lambs—and warm clothing, too!

I'm happy when we keep a few of the lambs. These two will probably stay with us for a few years.

This sheep looks ready for a haircut!

SHEEP
Give Us Wool

All sheep have wool on their bodies. Wool keeps them warm and dry. Since we keep our breeding sheep for a long time, they get their wool cut once a year. Cutting the wool is called **shearing**. Just like when you get a haircut, shearing doesn't hurt the sheep at all.

A family of shearers comes to Grandma's farm at the end of June. First they hold the sheep, so the sheep's feet are off the ground and its body stays very still. Then the shearers use a pair of sharp electric **shears** to cut off the wool. (The shearers cut the wool really close to the skin.) They start at the head of the sheep and go straight down its back. Then they shave the sides of the sheep. Next come the back, legs, and finally the belly. The shearers work fast! In less than ten minutes, the wavy wool from the sheep is on the ground. When the wool is all cut, it is in one piece. Now it is called **fleece**. One fleece can weigh up to 20 pounds!

I love to watch the shearers
cut the wool off our sheep.

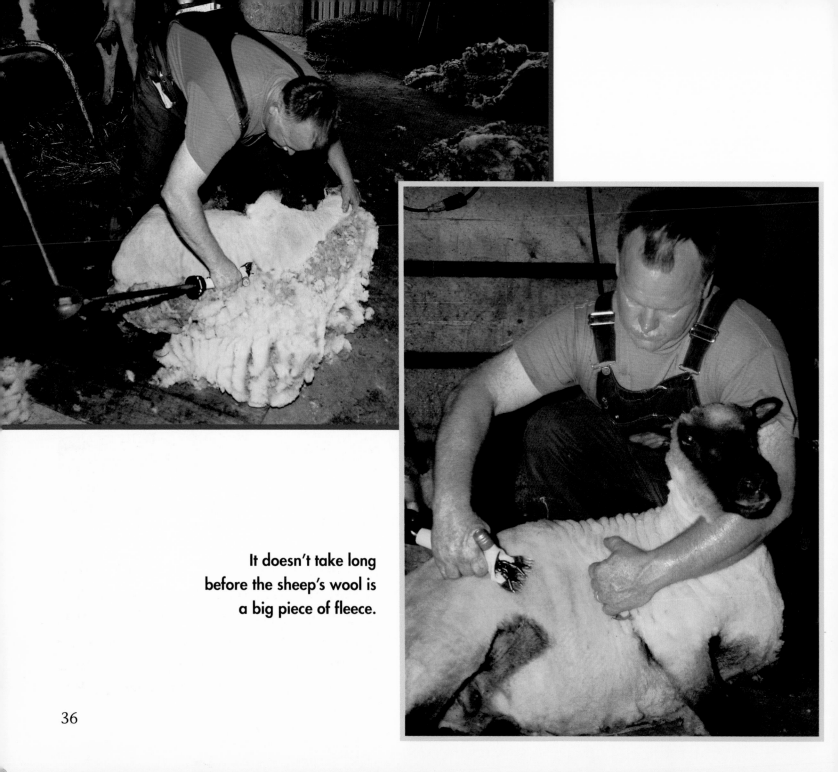

It doesn't take long
before the sheep's wool is
a big piece of fleece.

36

This fleece could someday make a sweater or a pair of warm socks!

We throw each sheep's fleece on a big table. There we straighten the fleece out. We also take out the short, dirty wool and remove any wool that breaks apart. When we're done, we tie a string around the fleece and stuff it into a big sack. Then Grandma sends the sack to a wool mill to be washed. The washing removes dirt, grease, and grass. After that, the wool is shipped to another mill. There it is made into yarn and dyed in many colors. In a few weeks, Grandma gets her yarn back.

Using knitting needles and her loom, Grandma makes sweaters, placemats, and tablecloths with her colorful yarn. She sells a lot of these items at her small shop, located right on the sheep farm.

She also sells blankets, hats, mittens, ties, and socks that she orders from other companies. Grandma enjoys working in her shop, and she likes to talk to people who come to visit.

Grandma makes beautiful things on her loom.

I hope one day I can knit as well as Grandma.

Grandma has been knitting for a long time.
She's really good at what she does.

Groups of kids visit our farm. They like to see what goes on here and, of course, see the sheep.

During the year, Grandma gives tours of the farm, too. She especially likes to do this in the spring, when the little lambs are here. During this time, she also gives demonstrations in her shop. She shows people how to spin wool to make yarn and how to weave yarn to make fabric.

Grandma also gives private spinning, weaving, and knitting lessons. For spinning and weaving lessons, she uses her five looms and four spinning wheels. One wheel, used just for show, is more than one hundred years old. It is called a "walking wheel." To use it, one has to stand and walk back and forth to spin the wool.

Here's Grandma at the walking wheel. Since this wheel is so old, it's very fragile. We have to be careful with it.

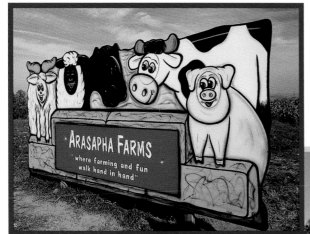

I like helping Grandma raise sheep on her farm.
We work hard, but we have lots of fun, too!

I hope someday I can take over Grandma's sheep farm. I look forward to living and working here for many more years. When I have children, I hope they raise their own animals. Then they can carry on the Bates family tradition!

42

Working on the sheep farm is part of our family tradition.

Fun Facts about SHEEP

SHEEP MILK CAN BE USED TO MAKE CHEESE AND YOGURT.

IN MANY COUNTRIES, PEOPLE DRINK MILK FROM SHEEP.

There are **45 different breeds** of **sheep** in the United States.

SHEEP are raised all over the country, but more are found in TEXAS than in any other state.

LANOLIN IS THE NATURAL OIL IN SHEEP'S WOOL. IT IS USED IN LOTIONS TO HELP KEEP SKIN SOFT.

A sheep gives an average of 7.7 pounds of fleece each year.

A EWE CAN LIVE TO BE ABOUT 14 YEARS OLD. If she has twins every year, she could have 28 lambs in her lifetime.

SHEEP ARE GOOD LAWN MOWERS — **THEY LOVE TO EAT GRASS!**

Learn More about SHEEP

Books

Miller, Sara Swan. *Sheep*. New York: Children's Press, 2000. This book describes the history of sheep and the life of modern sheep. You'll learn what the personality of a sheep is like, as well as favorite breeds and what makes these breeds so amazing.

Murray, Peter. *Sheep*. Chanhassen, MN: The Child's World, Inc., 1998. What is the food called that a sheep burps up from its stomach? Do you know what a fat-tailed breed of sheep looks like? Do all sheep have horns? Find answers to these and more!

Sloat, Teri. *Farmer Brown Shears His Sheep: A Yarn about Wool*. New York: DK Publishing, Inc., 2000. Farmer Brown shears his sheep, only to leave them out in the cold. They're shivering and need their fleece back! They follow the farmer, and find out what happens to the wool—how it's washed, combed and carded, then spun and dyed into yarn.

Websites

American Sheep Industry Association
<http://www.sheepusa.org>
Here's a place for people who are serious about sheep! This site includes sheep facts, animal health information, and news about the sheep industry. Click on the "For Kids" section to find cool facts about sheep, lambs, and wool. This section also gives links to other sites about agriculture.

Farm Animals for Kids and Teachers
<http://www.kiddyhouse.com/farm>
This colorful site features lots of activities and facts related to sheep and other farm animals. Listen to animal sounds, print out color pages and games, and sing animal songs along with music.

Kidz Korner
<http://www.mda.state.mi.us/kids/main.html>
Want to have fun while you learn all about agriculture? Visit a county fair and play games, do a word puzzle, and take an ice cream personality test. Also read stories about kids' lives on different kinds of farms.

National 4-H Council
<http://www.fourhcouncil.edu>
This fact-filled site will tell you everything about 4-H. Learn about this organization's programs, news, and local activities.

GLOSSARY

breed: to help a ewe become pregnant

colostrum: a mother's first milk, rich with vitamins and minerals

dock: to take a lamb's tail off, so the lamb stays clean and healthy

ewes: female sheep

fleece: wool coat from a sheep

4-H: a worldwide organization that helps kids learn skills and explore careers. The four H's stand for head, heart, hands, and health.

lamb: a baby sheep; to give birth

lambing pens: stalls where ewes give birth

mucus: a slippery coating that covers a newborn lamb's body

nurse: to drink milk from a mother's body

rams: male sheep

settled: pregnant

shearing: to cut or remove wool

shears: a sharp tool used for cutting or trimming

teat: a small, raised part on a mother ewe's belly through which a young sheep drinks milk

udder: the part of a ewe that makes milk

umbilical cord: the lifeline that connects a mother and baby while the baby grows inside the mother

wean: to stop drinking milk from a mother

yearlings: female sheep that haven't given birth yet

INDEX

About the AUTHOR

Judy Wolfman is a writer and professional story-teller, who teaches workshops on storytelling, creativity, and writing. She also enjoys writing and acting for the theater. She has published three children's plays, numerous magazine articles, short stories, poems, finger plays, and Carolrhoda's Life on a Farm series. A retired schoolteacher, Ms. Wolfman has two sons, a daughter, and four granddaughters. She lives in York, Pennsylvania.

About the PHOTOGRAPHER

David Lorenz Winston is an award-winning photographer whose work has been published by *National Geographic World*, UNICEF, and the National Wildlife Federation. In addition to his work on the Life on a Farm series, Mr. Winston has photographed farm animals for many years. He has also taught elementary school. In his spare time, he enjoys playing the piano at his home in southeastern Pennsylvania.